RALPH BAKSHI

and

The Lord of the Rings

sp

First published in 2001
ScreenPress Books
11 Buckshorn Lane
Eye
Suffolk
IP23 7AZ

Cover designed by Supärama Supämonkey
Designed by Sarah Theodosiou
Printed and bound by Omnia Books Limited

James Oliver is hereby identified as the author of this work in accordance with
Section 77 of the Copyright, Designs and Patents Act 1988

A CIP catalogue record for this book is available from the British Library
ISBN 1 901680 64 9

For information on forthcoming titles from ScreenPress Books please contact the
publisher's at the address above, fax: 01379 870267
or e-mail: mail@screenpress.co.uk

www.screenpress.co.uk

CONTENTS

INTRODUCTION

At the time of writing, the animated film of *The Lord of the Rings* is the most frequently requested home video title in the UK. Exclude the trilogies manufactured by Messrs Spielberg and Lucas, which have yet to appear in the new format, and the same is true of DVD as well. Even in the face of the extraordinary anticipation generated by the new live-action films directed by Peter Jackson, there is still considerable interest in the earlier animated version, which for some readers of the novel will always be the definitive interpretation.

This continuing fascination is all the more remarkable when you consider that the film has virtually no mainstream profile. Due to the rarity of screenings and the limited availability of video copies, it remains comparatively unknown outside its fan base. If it is remembered at all among the wider film-watching public, it is for the dubious honour of being the great unfinished cartoon.

Consequently, it is one of the few films that genuinely deserve the tag 'cult movie', having slowly built up a loyal cadre of fans away from the orthodox lists of 'classics' and critical approval. Like all the best cult movies, it polarizes audiences who have seen it, arousing strong passions. Some hate it, yet even the most vociferous detractors must admit that it contains sequences of enormous power and remains a brave and bold representation of J. R. R. Tolkien's book. On the other hand, even the most devoted fans cannot deny that the film has narrative shortcomings and is a highly idiosyncratic piece of work.

It is these contrasts that make the film so interesting. The tensions that Ralph Bakshi established between his determination to be as true to Tolkien's vision as he could and the need to change that vision to fit the confines of the cinema screen result in a film that frequently alternates between the brilliant and the baffling, sometimes within a single scene. Even after the recent proliferation of the form, there is still no other animated film quite like it – a dark fantasy for adults.

This book represents the first attempt to describe the processes that led to the shaping of the film, documenting the stages that the story went through on its way to the screen and how the film became a separate entity, distinct from the book. The story of how Tolkien wrote *The Lord of the Rings* has been told many times; the story of how Bakshi made his film version has not.

Sadly, this cannot be the definitive account. Ralph Bakshi declined to participate in interviews to discuss the project and so the ultimate story of the first *Lord of the Rings* film remains to be written. Indeed, coverage of all Bakshi's projects is long overdue. He was one of the most contentious and controversial figures in American cinema in the 1970s. The work he did and the positions he took have been extremely influential but remain largely undocumented. His films are difficult to obtain, especially outside the USA, yet he still has a fearsome cult reputation.

The animated *Lord of the Rings* is one of the great overlooked cult movies. The story of how it came to be made, and of the unorthodox way in which Bakshi chose to animate it, is intriguing in itself, but also means that the film will always warrant serious attention in its own right and not simply as a forerunner to later versions.

Long ago in the early years of the Second Age, the great Elven smiths forged rings of power. Nine for mortal men, seven for the Dwarf lords, three for the tall Elf-Kings. But then, the Dark Lord learned the craft of ring-making and made the master ring, the one ring to rule them all. With the one ring, Middle Earth is his and he cannot be overcome.

As the last alliance of men and elves fell beneath his power, he did not notice the heroic shadow who slipped in. It was Prince Isildur of the mighty kings from across the sea who took the ring. But because he did not destroy it, the spirit of the Dark Lord lived on and began to take shape and grow again. But the ring had a will of its own and a way of slipping from one hand to be found by another so that it might at last get back to its master.

The Dark Lord captured the nine rings that were made for men and turned their owners into Ring Wraiths, terrible shadows under his great shadow who roamed the world searching for the one ring!

Prologue to The Lord of the Rings by Peter S. Beagle and Chris Conkling

JOURNEY TO THE SCREEN

Appropriately in the light of the story it would tell, a film version of *The Lord of the Rings* appeared only after an epic journey. As history has shown, everything connected with the ring takes time. J. R. R. Tolkien had spent a lifetime dreaming about the mythologies and languages that inspired him; fourteen years were spent transmuting these obsessions into his gigantic saga. The result of his labours was so long that it had to be published as three separate volumes. It took time for them to connect with an audience, but the books gently snowballed in popularity and within a decade – not so very long really – the ageing Oxford don found himself the most popular fiction writer of his age.

As happens with all best-sellers, interest was expressed in converting the books to films, so as to make the most of their popularity, but Tolkien was cautious, realizing that the epic nature of his work would not fit easily within the confines of a traditional motion picture. For him (and many of his fans), the essence of *The Lord of the Rings* was to be found in the maps, the songs, the histories – the details and textures that would be the first things jettisoned by any screenwriter. 'You can't cramp narrative into dramatic form,' Tolkien elaborated in 1966, discussing his reluctance to see his work filmed. 'It would be easier to film *The Odyssey*. Much less happens. Only a few storms.'

However, there were considerations above and beyond artistic integrity for an impoverished academic in the days before the royalties started to flow – the same considerations, in fact, that had led him to sell his original manuscript to his wealthier American counterparts at Marquette University. In a letter dated 11 September 1957, Tolkien spelled out what motivated his dealings with the film industry: '[We] have agreed our policy: Art or Cash.

Either very profitable terms indeed or absolute author's veto on objectionable features or alterations.'

From the very beginning, animation was considered the only way to realize the story on film, as the technology simply didn't exist to adequately render Middle Earth in live action. The first approach made to Tolkien to create an animated film impressed him. The sample illustrations he was shown were 'really astonishingly good', evocative of '[Arthur] Rackham rather than Disney', for whose works he had a 'heartfelt loathing'. (Incidentally, the agent liaising with Tolkien over the project went on to establish his own small niche in pop culture folklore. As the publisher of *Famous Monsters of Filmland*, Forrest J. Ackerman became a cult figure with fans of genre cinema.)

The proposed script by Morton Grady Zuckerman, though, failed to meet with Tolkien's approval. He sent a lengthy critique of the screenplay to Ackerman, listing his unhappiness with what Zuckerman had done. He was especially displeased by such interpolations as 'a fairy castle' and the inclusion of 'a great many eagles'. In his eyes, the story had 'simply been murdered'. Tolkien concluded with a penetrating analysis of the problems that have plagued adaptations: 'The canons of narrative art in any medium cannot be wholly different; and the failure of poor films is often precisely in exaggeration, and in the intrusion of unwarranted matter owing to not perceiving where the core of the original lies.' The proposal went no further.

So, having tried 'Art', Tolkien turned instead to 'Cash', trading the rights for as much as he could and leaving the film world to get on with its own affairs while he retreated back to his books, his languages and correspondence with avid fans. He died in 1973 and, aside from some illicit student stage productions and tentative radio dramas, he never lived to see his work translated into another narrative medium.

Still the books kept selling, and more and more producers became interested in turning them into films, especially after the emergent counterculture of the 1960s co-opted the decidedly strait-laced Professor Tolkien as an unwilling guru. Tolkien's story became ever more popular and his sales shot through the roof. But despite the size of his fan base, no film materialized. In 1962 William L. Snyder's Rembrandt Films obtained the rights to *The Hobbit* and began work on the film the following year, but the project collapsed under its own financial weight and the rights were sold on again. Work on *The Lord of the Rings* never even reached that advanced stage: producers took out options on the material that quickly lapsed with nothing to show for their efforts. A consensus was gradually forming that the books were 'unfilmable', even as animation.

In the proverbial parallel universe, blighted by none of the problems that affect our own, all these unmade versions of *The Lord of the Rings* are playing at the same multiplex. A surprising number feature the voice of Orson Welles as Gandalf, appropriate casting given his love of magic and illusion. One version stars Leonard Nimoy from *Star Trek*, a keen reader of Tolkien's books. Most are animation, although a few brave producers have attempted live action, featuring a cast of thousands (and a budget of millions). The names of the producers and directors responsible for most of these films will be unfamiliar to even the most dedicated film buffs in the audience; most of them used *The Lord of the Rings* as an opportunity to break into the big time. But the most intriguing film showing at this hypothetical cinema features some very recognizable talent. Entitled *The Hobbits*, it stars – their first film since *Help!* – the Beatles.

Like all good hippies, the Beatles had read *The Lord of the Rings* and been enchanted by it. The idea to do something more with the book came from Dennis O'Dell, an executive of Apple Corp., the company established by the Beatles to release records, make films and change the world. Shortly after the release of *Sgt. Pepper's Lonely Hearts Club Band* in 1967, O'Dell proposed producing a version of Tolkien's story starring the Fab Four. The group were enthusiastic. Not only did they like the idea but it would also fulfil their contractual obligation to United Artists for a third and final film – UA had been pressing them for some months. Ideas were kicked about and casting discussed. Paul

GANDALF INSPECTS THE RING

The door opens.

FRODO: Gandalf!

GANDALF: Greetings, Frodo.

FRODO: Gandalf, it's really you! Oh, it's been so long!

GANDALF: Seventeen years since Bilbo left. You look the same as ever.

FRODO: You look older, Gandalf.

GANDALF: Oh, I've been on a long journey.

FRODO: It's the ring, isn't it? Bilbo's funny magic ring. You always used to look like that when you talked about it.

GANDALF: Bilbo's funny ring...that makes you invisible? Give it to me, Frodo.

FRODO: Give you the ring?

GANDALF: For a moment only.

Gandalf takes the ring.

GANDALF: Can you see any markings on it?

FRODO: There are none. It's quite a plain ring, really.

The wizard throws the ring on to the roaring fire, to Frodo's astonishment. The young Hobbit moves to retrieve it but is restrained by Gandalf.

GANDALF: Wait. Do you desire it so much already?

FRODO: No, but...but why ruin it?

GANDALF: Because it is altogether...evil. It will corrupt and destroy anyone who wears it...until he passes into the world of shadows, under the power of Sauron, the Dark Lord of Mordor!

McCartney would play Frodo, with Ringo Starr as his faithful retainer, Sam Gamgee. Because of his keen interest in mysticism, George Harrison was cast by the others as the wizard Gandalf, while John Lennon, the pin-up of millions, chose to play poor pathetic Gollum.

Unlike most of the earlier proposals, this would be a live-action film, and the Beatles were thinking big – bigger than Richard Lester, who had directed the earlier Beatles films. The first director approached was David Lean, who had proved his ability to tell a story on an epic canvas. Lean was interested but was immersed in pre-production for *Ryan's Daughter* and was unable to commit to the project. The next director invited to take charge of the project was Stanley Kubrick, director of Lennon's favourite film, *2001: A Space Odyssey*. Kubrick hadn't read the books and wasn't interested anyway. (At the time he was developing his own soon-to-be-aborted project, a biopic of Napoleon.) Finally, a world-class director agreed: Michelangelo Antonioni, the famed art-house idol who had mythologized swinging London in *Blow-Up*. To undertake the special effects, animator Ray Harryhausen was suggested.

However, as with so many of the projects the Beatles undertook after the death of Brian Epstein, this one came to nothing. In 1968 the group was in disarray, with the sessions for what was to become *The White Album* taking their toll on morale. Apple was a chaotic organization that haemorrhaged money on a series of ideas that had seemed promising at the start – a boutique, a state of the art recording studio – but lacked the formal structure that might have bought them to fruition. By the time O'Dell discovered that someone else had bought the film rights, the group's interest had waned and he was not able to get a clear commitment to pursue the matter further. The project fizzled out and for their third film United Artists got the documentary *Let It Be*, which showed the Beatles imploding.

Ironically, the person who had bought the rights had done so on behalf of United Artists, for $250,000. Had communication between the two camps been better, things might have been different, but in reality no one outside the group themselves knows what they would have made of *The Lord of the Rings*. Even without the Beatles, though, UA were keen to make the film and it was at their studios that most progress was made. They had the resources to fund the sort of long-term script development that would be necessary, not to mention renew their option while it was taking place. All earlier attempts had been by untried independents who lacked the resources of a major studio.

United Artists were also fortunate in their timing. By 1969 the novel had crossed over from cult to full-blown phenomenon. Among the millions of imaginations being fired by it were big-name directors keen to bring it to the screen. The first script commissioned was an elegant treatment by playwright Peter Schaffer, but nothing came of this and the project went cold until John Boorman became involved. Boorman was an Englishman who had stormed America with a series of visionary films – *Point Blank, Hell in the Pacific* and *Deliverance* – turning himself into one of the hottest directors of the early 1970s in the process. His films had earned respect from the critics and, more importantly in Hollywood's eyes, money at the box office.

John Boorman was an exciting choice, perfectly suited to the material. His early films display a remarkable sensitivity to the environments in which he dropped his protagonists. *Point Blank*, for example, is relentlessly urban, the perfect setting for Lee Marvin's rampaging ghost, while the contrasting wilderness of *Deliverance* develops into a non-speaking character in the film. There was also a gradually expanding mysticism in Boorman's work, a primeval spirituality throwing shadows across his films. If ever there was a director perfectly suited to bring the wild mythology of Middle Earth to the screen, it was Boorman.

John Boorman's arrival on the project displaced another contender, animator Ralph Bakshi, who had been lobbying the studio to let him handle the project. Bakshi had come across the books as a teenager, some twenty years before, and had been drawn to the 'brilliance' of Tolkien: 'It's probably one of the greatest fantasies ever written. The language is perfect, the characterizations are perfect, the mood is perfect. There isn't a page of *Rings* that you wouldn't want to re-read a hundred times.'

THE LOYALTY OF HOBBITS

Having survived a near-assault by the Black Rider, Merry looks determined.

MERRY: We're going with you, Frodo.

FRODO: With me? But how do you...Sam...But you gave your word.

MERRY: Sam didn't tell us about the ring.

FRODO. I saw Bilbo use it once, before he went away...to hide from the Sackville-Bagginses. And after that, Pippin and I kept on the lookout, and we followed you and we asked questions everywhere.

PIPPIN: And we even wormed a few things out of Gandalf.

FRODO: And you spied on me and Sam helped you.

MERRY: And we spied on you.

SAM: But we meant no harm to you, Mr Frodo. Don't you remember what Mr Gandalf said? 'Take someone who you can trust,' he said.

FRODO: It doesn't seem to me that I can trust anyone.

MERRY: It all depends on what you want. You can trust us to stick with you through thick and thin to the bitter end! But you cannot trust us to let you face trouble alone and go off without a word. We're your friends, Frodo.

And he was convinced that the only way that it could be filmed was as animation. But there were no opportunities for him to do anything while John Boorman was involved.

Meanwhile, to muddy the waters further, it should be noted that United Artists didn't own all the rights to Tolkien's work. Due to a legal oversight, UA didn't hold the television rights and these were eventually picked up by a small company who specialized in animation for television, Rankin/Bass. They produced two films that capitalized on the fully authorized film version. The first, an adaptation of *The Hobbit*, featured the voices of film directors John Huston and Otto Preminger. The same cast reprised their roles for an adaptation of *The Return of the King*, shown shortly after the UA film was finally released. The quality is low, but their mere existence has caused consternation and confusion among fans wondering about film versions of Tolkien's books.

When Boorman returned with a finished script, the executives at United Artists were shocked by what they saw. According to Ralph Bakshi, he had collapsed the trilogy into a single script; it was over 700 pages long and filled with language that the suits couldn't understand, mainly because they had never read the books on which it was based. A rough costing of the script further prejudiced the studio against the project, which they deemed would be prohibitively expensive. They chose not to finance the John Boorman film. Elements of his script filtered into his later films, most notably *Excalibur*, another story of quests and magic, but otherwise the project is entombed for ever in the script archives of United Artists.

Into this vacuum stepped Ralph Bakshi. He pointed out to the studio that they owned the rights to a property with huge commercial potential, a vast fan base and name recognition among those who hadn't even read the books. Any live-action film would suffer from budgetary problems, whereas animation was much more flexible and infinitely cheaper. His pitch made a lot of sense to the executives, who were impressed by his enthusiasm. He got the job.

RALPH BAKSHI

Enthusiasm for Tolkien's work would never have been enough on its own to persuade United Artists to entrust Ralph Bakshi with such a potentially lucrative property as *The Lord of the Rings*. The studio was well aware of the need to attract heavyweight talent if it was to bring the film to fruition and track record was held to be all-important. Bakshi was given the green light based on his previous box-office success.

One of the foremost animators of his generation, his reputation was based on a group of films that had dragged animation kicking and screaming out of its traditional place as wholesome family entertainment. Tackling contemporary issues, the films were relentlessly harsh: forget the gentle lyricism of Walt Disney, Bakshi made the cartoon equivalent of Brooklyn on a Saturday night. And they had made money – a lot of money.

This background might not have made him an immediately obvious choice for the *Lord of the Rings* project, but he claimed to understand Tolkien's books in a way that the studio executives didn't. It was decided that his abrasive intelligence would give the film textures that mainstream animators could never hope to match.

Ralph Bakshi was born on 26 October 1938 in Haifa, now part of Israel, then part of Palestine. His Russian parents moved from the Middle East to America and Ralph was brought up in poverty in Brownsville, Brooklyn. His formative years in the slums of New York not only influenced his work and his approach to it, they also provided the direct inspiration for his second feature film, *Heavy Traffic*.

At eighteen, Bakshi left Manhattan High School for the Industrial Arts for a job at the Terrytoons cartoon studio. He'd grown up with animation and loved the form. He aspired to create his own films, personal projects away from the talking animals and super-heroes he was surrounded by at work, but first he had to learn the basics. He started as a paint opaquer and gradually impressed his employers enough to gain promotion. (It was around this time that he first read Tolkien.) By the time he was twenty-six, he had earned his animator's wings and was working on such Saturday morning fare as *Heckle & Jeckle* and *Deputy Dawg*. In 1966 he was appointed director of the entire studio.

No twenty-eight-year-old in 1966 wanted to be crafting low-budget, low-quality children's television. This was the era of social protest and youth rebellion, two things close to Ralph Bakshi's heart. He was getting frustrated at the conservative nature of the medium he was working in. 'All the animation I ever saw was a fantasy or fairy-tale orientation,' he told an interviewer. 'I wanted to make films closer to myself.' In another interview, he went further: 'The animation industry, unlike other forms of entertainment, has never crept up from its origins in terms of subject matter. Animation in America has never tried to change.' No wonder he wasn't thrilled about his latest project: directing the first episodes of the animated Spiderman series.

An opportunity to step off the Terrytoons conveyor belt presented itself and Bakshi took it. He was appointed head of Paramount's New York-based cartoon studio. But no sooner had he taken up his post than Paramount's owners, Gulf + Western, decided to cut costs by shutting the cartoon studio down and he was out of a job. But his time had not been completely unproductive. Bakshi had met producer Steve Krantz during his brief tenure and, faced with unemployment, they decided instead to begin raising money for what was to be one of the most influential – and profitable – animated films ever made.

Superficially, *Fritz the Cat* looks like any other cartoon film. After all, the eponymous hero is an anthropomorphized animal, strutting around, walking and talking just like a human being. But there the similarities end, because, unlike his rivals, this tom-cat wasn't neutered. Derived from the cult cartoon strip by R. Crumb, the film follows Fritz's encounters with Hell's Angels, the police

THE COUNCIL OF ELROND

BOROMIR: What foolishness is this? Why do you speak of hiding in this story? This ring could save all Middle Earth.

ELROND: Have you heard nothing? It is Sauron's ring...to wield it, you would have to become Sauron. I will not touch it.

GANDALF: Nor I. Our one hope lies in foolishness, Boromir. The Dark Lord cannot conceive of anyone wishing to destroy his ring. He will wait until one of us tries to use it, follow every move we make, and it is just possible that he may not notice the small quiet feet walking into peril in Mordor.

BILBO: Very well, very well. It's plain enough what you're pointing at. Bilbo, the silly Hobbit, started this affair and Bilbo had better finish it...or himself. When ought I to start?

GANDALF: It has passed beyond you, Bilbo. This last journey must be for others to make.

BILBO: Aaah, and who are they to be?

GANDALF: That is what they're trying to decide here.

FRODO: I will take the ring, though I do not know the way.

ELROND: I think that this task is appointed for you, Frodo. This is the hour of the Shire-folk at last.

and numerous sexual partners as he tries to 'find himself'. Frustrated by years of sanitized cartooning, Bakshi shot the works; the literally graphic depictions of drugs and group sex earned the picture an X certificate from the MPAA, unprecedented for an animated film.

Fritz the Cat cost $750,000 to make (at 1972 prices) and earned its budget back many times over. Exact grosses are difficult to come by, as the film earned much of its money in second-run houses and at midnight movie screenings, the spiritual home of Fritz himself. In terms of cost-to-profit ratio, it's still one of the most successful films ever made. Everyone who chipped in finance made a lot of money. Not everyone liked it. Robert Crumb wasn't happy with what Bakshi did to his creation, and traditional animators were appalled for the very reasons that made Bakshi a cult hero with the younger generation. But why should Bakshi care? He'd managed to do what he had always wanted and make a cartoon for grown-ups.

Having liberated the content of animated features, Bakshi's next project was the first to challenge their form. *Heavy Traffic* was ostensibly an autobiographical film about a young kid of immigrant parents growing up in a Brooklyn neighbourhood who dreams of becoming a cartoonist. (As with *Fritz the Cat*, Bakshi didn't pull his punches: the film has something to offend everyone, from hard-core porn to homophobia via killing God.) None of the money from *Fritz the Cat* trickled down to the budget, which was again minuscule. The financial difficulties led Bakshi to employ cost-cutting methods, but he actually became intrigued by these and began to use them as stylistic devices in their own right.

Specifically, Bakshi became entranced by the creative possibilities of the Rotoscope. Rotoscoping is a technique whereby frames of live-action footage are traced over and converted into animation. It was a technique that was to be used extensively during the production of *The Lord of the Rings* and will therefore be discussed more thoroughly there. *Heavy Traffic* saw only a comparatively small use of the technique for its own sake and marked the beginning of Bakshi's move away from pure animation to try and create something entirely new. 'I want to do everything live action can do and then do everything live action can't do,' he said. 'I want to create a new image.'

Warming to his theme, Bakshi elaborated in typically pugnacious style. 'Let's clear up where I'm going. I don't give a *fuck* for animation as it's been done. I'm looking for a new medium. I'm looking for total realism, with all the nuances...My job in my medium is to create an *emotion* on the screen that is an emotion. I don't care how I get there.' (His interest in marrying live action and animation climaxed in 1992 with *Cool World*, his last feature to date, which merged the two forms.)

Bakshi's words sound eerily prescient, anticipating the situation created by the revolution in computer graphics which has rendered the distinction between live action and animation arbitrary. Look at *Star Wars: The Phantom Menace* or even Peter Jackson's film of *The Lord of the Rings*, live-action films that blend the photographed image with computer-generated animations. But Bakshi was speaking nearly thirty years ago, before computers, and his attitude put him on a collision course with the animation community. The old guard were horrified by his subject matter and his vulgarity, while the younger generation were up in arms because of his bold apostasy over technique.

He made enemies easily. Sci-fi writer Ray Bradbury said of him, 'He's the only man I've ever seen who hates everybody.' (Bakshi, in turn, commented, 'I heard that when Ray Bradbury saw *Heavy Traffic*, he almost fell out of the screening room.') Chuck Jones, the father of Daffy Duck, expressed similar sentiments in more moderate language. Animation journals fulminated against him as a heretic. But, as Bakshi was to find, these were just warm-up bouts. The main event was still to come.

With the understatement and euphemism characteristic of the format, the production notes for *The Lord of the Rings* describe Bakshi's third feature thus: 'Coonskin, an animated film, was also politically motivated. It was not widely distributed commercially but has attained a cult following.' What this (broadly correct) outline fails to convey is even a fraction of controversy that greeted Bakshi as a result of his movie, one of the most provocative, inflammatory and offensive (either animation *or* live action) ever made.

Coonskin – and no, the title doesn't refer to Davy Crockett's fur cap – is a tough film in every respect. It deals with very sensitive issues in a very insensitive way. In it, the director tackles the most divisive issue in America, racism, head on and fist first. Broadly speaking, the film is a parody of the Uncle Remus stories of Joel Chandler Harris and more specifically the film adaptation of them, *Song of the South*, produced (and currently suppressed in America) by Disney. It aimed to rip apart the hypocritical, patronizing portrayal of black people in American culture and openly confront the racism of that society. Having grown up on the streets, Bakshi felt very close to the black position and wanted to start a debate.

'I decided to do a film…describing what has gone down with black people, what is the folk art that has produced the black lifestyle, and to write a modern-day folk tale about the position that blacks are in now, using old and new symbols.' That was Bakshi's stated ambition, but it wasn't his aims that got him into trouble, rather his methods, which involved ugly caricatures and potentially offensive symbolism.

Coonskin first attracted the attention of the Congress of Racial Equality (CORE) because of the title, which the director had always meant ironically. But intentions are not always clear and CORE objected. Bakshi conceded the point but his producer, Al Ruddy, disagreed. '[He] said, "No, no one is changing the title. It would look like we sold out",' remembered Bakshi. 'I said, "Al, change the title. It's the interior of the picture I care about."' But Ruddy resisted the pressure. When CORE did see the interior of the picture, they increased their objections.

Bakshi was discovering the hard way that one man's satire is another man's blasphemy. In making a film denouncing racism, he had left himself open to charges that he was a racist himself. He had filled his film with images he had clearly intended to be parodic, images that drew on the offensive clichés about appearance and behaviour. But CORE couldn't see the joke in recycling depictions it had spent a long time trying to bury and was saying so loudly in no uncertain terms.

When the film was shown at the Museum of Modern Art in New York, CORE activists invaded the screening and publicly branded Bakshi a racist in front of a genuinely mixed audience. In the ensuing mêlée outside the museum, Bakshi was beaten up. Not everyone sided with CORE. The National Association for the Advancement of Colored People viewed the film and agreed that it was an attack on racism rather than actually racist. (The NAACP itself had been founded in direct response to a racist film, D. W. Griffith's *Birth of a Nation*.) But the film proved too controversial for Paramount, the distributing studio, and it was quietly dumped.

Bakshi practically lost his shirt in the fiasco, which had the knock-on effect of sabotaging his next project. *Hey Good Lookin'* was halfway to completion when Warner Brothers got cold feet at the depictions of racial violence. They objected to a scene where a white gang fights a black gang. It didn't matter to them that it was only incidental – any controversy was too much for them. Ironically, *Coonskin* was finally released on video without anyone complaining – maybe because the title had been changed to the thoroughly innocuous *Street Fight*, just as Bakshi had wanted from the beginning.

Coonskin wasn't the last of Bakshi's 'urban' films. After finishing *The Lord of the Rings*, he made *American Pop*, a spiritual sibling of *Heavy Traffic*, looking at rock and roll in America. But although clearly related, the film was mellower than its predecessors. Bakshi seemed less willing to start fights.

This was evident in the project that did eventually follow *Coonskin*, *Wizards*. It began as an elliptical examination of the forces that led to the creation of the state of Israel, but Bakshi swaddled his potentially controversial thesis in fantasy, as a post-apocalyptic sword and sorcery film showing the battle of two brothers. It was the first film directed by Bakshi that wasn't given an X certificate, sporting a family-friendly PG instead. With a budget of only $1.5 million, the film went on to gross $20 million. Of course, with the exception of *Coonskin*, every Bakshi film had been a gold mine.

And that's what sold the United Artists executives on the idea of a Ralph Bakshi-directed *Lord of the Rings*. He knew what the kids wanted. In his mid-1970s prime, he was a serious threat to Disney, which had been in the doldrums since the death of Uncle Walt. They had the money for lavish animation and the heritage to exploit, but their new films just weren't connecting. Yet here was Bakshi, tearing up the rulebook, living hand to mouth, producing ramshackle animation and making millions!

Ralph Bakshi is certainly an influential figure in the development of animation. He was the first commercial animator to challenge the Disney aesthetic that had dominated for so many years. Even if there is no direct influence, today's generation of adult animations – *Beavis and Butthead*, *South Park* – work in the territory first explored by Ralph Bakshi. Indeed, *Ren & Stimpy* owe their existence to Bakshi, as it was he who promoted their creator, John Kricfalusi, to director and mentored the young animator for many years.

Bakshi saw himself paralleling in animation what Martin Scorsese, another New York film-maker, was doing in live action. A retrospective of Bakshi's films showed that his work from the early 1970s still had the power to shock. He was pleased: 'Well, so does *Raging Bull* and *Taxi Driver*. That's the generation I grew up with. I just happened to be an animator.' But the crucial distinction was that Scorsese had precedents for what he was doing, while Bakshi was breaking new ground, often aggressively. His struggle for respectability was harder.

Summarizing himself, Bakshi says, 'If you have to pin down what drives me, it's freedom. The right to make choices, the fact that no one tells you what to do.' Asked about his attitude to his work, he responded with a quote that acts as an excellent summary of the man and his movies: 'I can't be friends with everyone. I respond negatively to what people say and do. They have their rights. Just don't tell me what to make.'

THE ELVEN SONG OF MITHRANDIR

Let the night never cease to call you
Let the day never more be the same
Where you go
Will we try to follow
Will we try to follow
We're still guided by your light
You're walking beside us
A prayer in the night
With the fear rushing
Through the shadows like a star
Shining deep in his heart
You will know in your hearts for ever
Never more will we stand alone

THE SCREENPLAY

After making the deal to create *The Lord of the Rings*, Ralph Bakshi's first decision was to invite Saul Zaentz on board. He knew he'd need a producer to help him make the picture, someone to cover his back against the studio, and Zaentz was an obvious choice. Zaentz was an experienced producer who had first encountered Bakshi when he was one of the investors who'd had a small stake converted into a windfall by the runaway success of *Fritz the Cat*. More pertinently, he had become a good friend to the animator.

Zaentz was a late arrival to the film industry. Born in New York, he drifted west after the Second World War and became involved in the music industry, eventually heading his own record label. His was the first company to produce albums by controversial comedian Lenny Bruce, although it was jazz musicians like Dave Brubeck who were responsible for most of his success. As rock and roll displaced jazz, Zaentz's canny instincts lead him to sign Creedence Clearwater Revival and make another fortune as they went on to sell millions. (The relationship eventually soured and in the 1980s Zaentz was involved in protracted litigation with Creedence's leader, John Fogerty.)

Aged fifty-seven, Zaentz decided to move into film-making. The showmanship and hustling skills he had acquired in the record business would serve him well. In his attitude to movies, Zaentz is a throwback to the early days when producers took real risks. He never gets involved in a project unless he feels passionate about it and then shepherds it at every stage with microscopic attention to detail. The four Oscars on his mantelpiece (three Best Pictures and a Lifetime Achievement Award) are testament to his success. Anthony Minghella, who directed Zaentz's film *The English*

Patient, described the producer's approach as being like 'a bull patrolling the perimeter of the film at all times, keeping away his enemies and protecting his friends'.

His first major success was *One Flew Over the Cuckoo's Nest*, which earned him the first Best Picture nod, and it was the success of this film that led him to seriously consider Bakshi's offer. Just like *Cuckoo's Nest*, *The Lord of the Rings* was a cult book with an army of loyal fans. He also appreciated – and shared – Bakshi's maverick approach, both of them realizing that unconventional films could be good box office. He accepted the offer. Appropriately for the producer of *The Lord of the Rings*, Zaentz's company was called Fantasy Films.

There was one hurdle that had to be overcome. A true independent, Zaentz is involved with every aspect of his films, including the financing. None of his films (which also include *Amadeus* and *The Unbearable Lightness of Being*) have been financed by studios in the traditional way and, as a result, the producer has held an unprecedented degree of artistic control over production. If he was to be involved with Bakshi's film, he would arrange the financing. Fortunately, studios are always pleased to save money and United Artists were happy to negotiate a deal with Zaentz to turn the picture into an independent pick-up rather than a studio production. They sold him the film rights in exchange for world distribution rights (except for Australia, New Zealand and Sweden, where Zaentz had made separate arrangements with existing contacts). UA were thus protected from a potentially very expensive picture, while Zaentz and Bakshi had complete freedom to make their movie.

Before a writer had been engaged or any pre-production artwork drawn, Zaentz and Bakshi arranged a trip to England to meet with the Tolkien estate. J. R. R. Tolkien had died in 1973 but the two men met with his son Christopher and his publishers in order to reassure them of the purity of their intentions. The British contingent were more interested in preparing the late professor's unfinished writings for publication, but since their blessing seemed important to the Americans, they were happy to confer it upon the

IN THE GARDEN OF GALADRIEL

Sam and the Elven queen are talking.

GALADRIEL: This is the mirror of Galadriel. It shows things that were and things that are and things that yet may be. Do you wish to look?

SAM: I'm not one to glimpse what's goin' on at home. It seems a terrible long time I've been away.

GALADRIEL: Come then, you shall look and see what you may.

Sam looks and is shocked by what he sees.

SAM: I gotta go home! They've dug up Bagshot Row and thrown my poor old gaffer out in the street! I gotta go home!

GALADRIEL: The mirror shows many things, Sam, and not all have yet come to pass. Some never come to be...unless those that behold the visions turn aside from their path to prevent them. Do you wish to leave Frodo now and go home?

SAM: No.

Elsewhere in the garden, Frodo looks into the mystical pools and sees...

FRODO: Gandalf! No! No! It must be Aruman!

GALADRIEL: Do not touch the water! He is looking for you. But he cannot find you. Not here. Not yet. The door is closed.

FRODO: 'Three rings for the Elven Kings under the sky.'

GALADRIEL: Yes. We hid those three from him and he has never found them. If your quest fails, then nothing can stand against him and we are defenceless. Yet if you succeed, if the one ring is destroyed, all we built with the three will fade. Time will come here and Lothlorien will fade. You are the footstep of doom to us, Frodo.

FRODO: Lady Galadriel, I will give you the one ring if you ask for it. It's far too great a matter for me.

GALADRIEL: (laughing) And I came to test your heart! You will give me the great ring freely and in place of the Dark Lord you will set up a queen. And I shall not be evil but beautiful and terrible as the morning and the night, stronger than the foundations of the earth! All shall love me and despair! (pause) I pass the test. I will diminish and go into the west and remain Galadriel. And you must depart in the morning.

project. Zaentz also used the opportunity to purchase merchandising rights for the property, establishing a new company, Tolkien Enterprises, to handle sales based on J. R. R. Tolkien's writings.

Thus anointed by the Tolkien clan, production began in earnest on the film. The first stage was the preparation of a screenplay, an epic task in itself. The very nature of Tolkien's book – the sheer length, the intricate patterning of the storylines, the histories backed up by genealogies, maps and numerous appendices – worked against easy compression into screenplay format. No matter how pure Bakshi's intentions were, it would be simply impossible to make a film of *The Lord of the Rings* without dramatic alterations to the form and structure of the storyline.

From the start, both producer and director were agreed that there was no way of squeezing the book into a single film, so there would be two films; a full trilogy was decided against because of cost. Each would be produced separately, however. Creating five hours of animation would take too long and cost far too much, so it was decided to divide production of the two films.

The herculean labour of adapting the story into a screenplay was given to Chris Conkling. The son of a record producer, Conkling had recently returned to California after spending two years as a missionary in Japan. The first person to offer him a job was Ralph Bakshi, who needed a researcher/writer. Conkling's only previous experience as a writer had been a history book, *A Joseph Smith Chronology*, but Bakshi was impressed by his early work and Conkling began on the screenplay. It was perhaps unwise to assign such an enormous project to a novice. The resultant screenplay met with a cool response and, although he retains a credit on the film, Conkling contributed no more to the screenplay. A new writer was sought.

Peter S. Beagle remembers his first exposure to J. R. R. Tolkien: 'I first read W. H. Auden's front-page review of *The Lord of the Rings* in the *New York Times* book review in 1954 when I was fifteen. I already knew that Auden was a famous poet but I'd certainly never heard of J. R. R. Tolkien. The book sounded intriguing, but I couldn't ever find it, not in libraries, not in bookstores (though it must have been for sale), and I didn't know anyone who had seen or read it. It took me years to come across a copy at the Carnegie Library in Pittsburgh, where I was a junior at the university. I snatched up all three books, took them back to my room and was incommunicado for the next three or four days. I must have gone to classes but I swear I don't remember doing it. The impact was overwhelming at the time. There weren't any factory-produced epic fantasies crowding the racks in those days and I'd never read anything like this. Try to imagine explaining Tolkien's work in 1958. Nobody knew who the hell he was, and only a very few cared.'

By the time he read *The Lord of the Rings*, Peter Beagle was already an accomplished writer. His short stories had won awards and been published in magazines. He soon graduated from the short form to the novel, meeting with considerable acclaim. His first major success (and still the book he is best known for) was the gently beguiling fantasy *The Last Unicorn*. The book was later turned into an animated movie, ironically produced by Rankin/Bass, who held the TV rights to Tolkien's work.

In addition to creating his own worlds, Beagle continued to explore Tolkien's. He contributed to an anthology, *After the King*, in which a variety of authors wrote stories set in Middle Earth. In addition, he wrote forewords to two of the books in the trilogy itself and a lengthy article that appeared in *The Tolkien Reader*, a guide to Tolkien's writings. (Despite all this, he rejects the tag 'Tolkien scholar', which is frequently applied to him. 'I still get occasional letters written in Elvish [though]...') It was this, and specifically his work on *The Tolkien Reader*, that alerted Bakshi and Zaentz and led them to hire Beagle as consultant to the project.

However, as Beagle was to discover, more than simple consultation was required; in fact the script needed completely rethinking. It was a huge job. 'I was extremely daunted by the size of the project,' he remembers, 'but I was also inspired by one of the great anonymous screenwriter sayings: "If they ask you, you *can* write a song..."' Armed with that thought, Beagle sat down at his

BOROMIR'S MOMENT OF MADNESS

Frodo is lost in contemplation, away from the others in the fellowship, but he is soon aware that he is not alone.

FRODO: Who's – who's there?

It is Boromir.

Boromir!

BOROMIR: I was afraid for you, Frodo. The Orcs may be on this side of the river by now. May I stay and talk to you, just for a while?

FRODO: Oh, you're kind, but there's nothing to be said. I know what I should do, but I'm afraid of doing it, Boromir.

BOROMIR: I wish I could help you. Will you hear my counsel?

FRODO: I know what your advice would be, Boromir. To go with you to Gondor and use the ring to defend Minas Tirith.

BOROMIR: And is that such ill counsel? Why should we fear to use the ring in a just cause?

FRODO: Boromir, whatever is done with the ring turns to evil. Gandalf and Elrond refused to touch it...and Galadriel herself –

BOROMIR: Yes, yes. I know all that! And for themselves, they might be right. These Elves and half-elves and wizards! But true-hearted men will not be corrupted. We of Minas Tirith do not seek power. Only the strength to defend ourselves. Where is the evil in that, Frodo?

He receives no answer.

You cannot answer me. None of them can! It's madness not to use the power of the enemy against him. Think what Aragorn could do with the ring in this hour. Or if he refuses, why not Boromir? How I would drive the hosts of Mordor, until I stood face to face with Sauron himself. And they tell us to throw it away! Come with me, Frodo. My city is not far. You can go on to Mordor from there, if you must. Only trust me. Let me try my plan. Lend me the ring.

FRODO: No, Boromir, no!

BOROMIR: Fool! Obstinate fool! It is only yours by chance. It might have been mine. It should have been mine. Give it to me!

Startled by Boromir's aggression, Frodo takes the ring and puts it on his finger, vanishing immediately from sight.

Miserable trickster. You'll sell us all to Sauron. Traitor! Traitor! Curse you to death and darkness, all you Halflings!

But slowly he calms down and realizes what he has done.

What have I done? Frodo, come back! A madness took me but it has passed! Come back!

desk to write, rewrite and write again.

For all the professed devotion to Tolkien, Beagle was given a free hand in building the screenplay. 'No one ever expected me to capture the book's tone. That's pretty much impossible anyway when a book is translated into film; if you're very lucky you find a cinematic equivalent for the author's voice and style. Not impossible but fairly rare. As far as structure goes, events were moved around, altered or eliminated – witness Tom Bombadil – as thought necessary. I kept as much of Tolkien's original language as I could get away with, always bearing in mind that dialogue written to be read is different to dialogue intended to be spoken. But the issue of remaining "true to Tolkien" was never discussed. I can't remember being chided for changing or inventing something – at least not because I was blaspheming sacred writ. I can honestly say that I did not write the line "That's sort of a relief" for Frodo. That was most likely Ralph, and he'll undoubtedly pay for it in his next incarnation.'

In fact, the major concern during the development and refining of the screenplay was the length of the film. The average animated feature is around the ninety-minute mark. Bakshi's anxiety grew when he cast his eye over the mountain of pages he had to animate. '[He] was quite aware that [it] was undoubtedly going to be the longest animated film in history and it worried the hell out of him. When he discovered that King Theoden and the riders of Rohan would have to be kept in the story – a whole new people and culture to be introduced – he almost went straight round the bend. This relates to a greater inherent problem, which is that animation hates to stand still, especially for exposition, and when it comes to the history of Middle Earth and the rings, we're dealing with world-class exposition.'

The consequence of this problem is one of the flaws in the final film: the inconsistent use of history, which is never fully blended in with the rest of the storyline. The way that the history is used also assumes at least a working knowledge of the original books. The council at Rivendell is the severest example of this, due to the compression of over fifty pages of lengthy exposition into a little under five minutes.

Despite being originally hired as a consultant for a flat fee ('quite a small one'), Beagle was kept busy and was ultimately responsible for the entire screenplay, despite the shared credit. 'As far as how many drafts the script went through, I can't even guess. All I can answer after so many years is lots and lots. And then more lots.' Zaentz and Bakshi got excellent value for money from Peter Beagle, 'and it's been a sore point with my agent ever since'.

Beagle's original script ended with a title-card, 'Here ends the first part of *The Lord of the Rings*', and this was the version originally filmed and previewed. However, before the picture opened nation-wide, it was decided to alter the structure of the film by switching certain scenes in the final reels around to suggest that the story was completed. The title-card was dropped and replaced by the narration that now ends the film.

Beagle wasn't consulted about these changes and remains angry about them, as they damage all the work that had gone into the project. But he had left the film by the time this switch was pulled and could do nothing about it. Happy memories? 'I got a trip to England out of it, and the credit got me a lot of film and TV work for the next several years. Besides, Ralph introduced me to Japanese food and instilled in me a lifelong love of sashimi. Money or no money, it was worth it.'

PRODUCTION

The biggest problem Ralph Bakshi had to face wasn't which of the many stories in the book to tell but how to tell them. The difficulty of adapting any book for the screen is that film directors simply don't have the licence that authors do to allow readers to use their imagination. Film as a medium depends so much on the shared visual experience, in a way that writing, a much more personal and suggestive medium, doesn't; if something isn't defined on a cinema screen, in appearance and sound, then it simply doesn't exist for the viewer.

Bakshi was aware of the problems he faced. How could he possibly satisfy the millions of readers who each had their own, very personal conception of Middle Earth? He couldn't. All he could hope for was to impress them with his sincerity. 'My right to feel about it as a Tolkien fan is the same right that other Tolkien fans have. "You're a Tolkien fan doing it" is how I kept talking to myself,' he explained. 'When I used to go to Eberts Field to yell and scream for the Brooklyn Dodgers with 50,000 other people, as far as I was concerned, it was just me. They were winning it for me.' Such was also his approach to *The Lord of the Rings*.

Although Bakshi is American, he gave the film a very deliberate European aesthetic. The major influences on Tolkien were the northern European myths and legends; indeed, he considered Middle Earth essentially to be Europe, with the Shire being firmly in England and Mordor lying in the Balkans. But Bakshi's decision was based on his conception of the book as a 'European' story and he therefore chose to emphasize those elements, with one significant exception. The physical appearance of Strider is that of a Native American, albeit with an English accent.

Tolkien had provided illustrations for *The Hobbit* (but none for

The Lord of the Rings), revealing a little of the appearance of the world that he had created. A keen amateur artist, he had drawn pictures of Rivendell, the Shire and even the interior of a Hobbit hole. A brief examination of the film shows that although Bakshi chose not to emulate Tolkien's style of illustration, he used the illustrations as the basis of his own designs for the film's locations.

The film owes surprisingly little to the popular conventions of mythology as reflected in the sword and sorcery genre. Bakshi's approach for all of his animated features was to do as much research as possible and allow himself to be influenced by what he found. For *The Lord of the Rings*, rather than examine fantasy artwork filled with their muscle men and pneumatic women, he went back much further in time and looked at fifteenth-century engravings and paintings by the sixteenth- and seventeenth-century Dutch masters, especially Bruegel and Rembrandt. This is especially evident in the film's colour scheme, which is derived from Rembrandt's use of colour.

More typical of the fantasy genre, although certainly true to Tolkien, is the appearance of the film's two wizards, Gandalf and (S)Aruman (the character was renamed after preview audiences complained that both villains had names beginning with 'S' and they therefore got confused between Saruman and Sauron). The wizards' white beards are more luxuriant in the film than described in the book, as though patterned after pictures of the wizard Merlin. The aspects of the film that succeed most completely are the nightmare creatures of Mordor, the Ring Wraiths and the armies of Orcs. The Ring Wraiths in particular, with their bizarre shuffling gait, are an acknowledged highlight.

An unfortunate design aspect of the film, and one that could not have been foreseen at the time, is the way that contemporary fashions have been reflected in the film, dating it slightly. This is most noticeable in the hairstyles of the characters, especially the Hobbits, which are perhaps somewhat fuller than their creator might have approved of.

In an interview given before the film's release, Bakshi discussed his conception of the characters and explained how he approached

GOLLUM MEETS THE HOBBITS

The two Hobbits stand in isolation against the barren landscape of Mordor.

SAM: We're plain lost, Mr Frodo.

FRODO: Oh, I'm tired, Sam. I don't know what's to be done. We must find a place to camp, I suppose. Maybe there'll be a path tomorrow.

They are not to know that they are being stalked, followed by one of the ring's former owners, Gollum.

GOLLUM: Cautious, my precious.

Frodo has spotted their shadow and remembers the stories that Bilbo told him about the wretched creature.

FRODO: Don't turn! It's him.

SAM: That Gollum? The thing that had Mr Bilbo's ring?

FRODO: He's been following us since Moria, I think.

SAM: Well, he'll be sorry he found us again.

FRODO: Be careful, he's much more dangerous than he looks.

GOLLUM: Where is it, my precious? It's ours, it is, and we wants it.

Sam accosts Gollum and tussles with him. Frodo intervenes when the fight turns against Sam.

FRODO: Let go, Gollum. Let go or I'll cut your throat.

GOLLUM: Don't hurt us! Don't let them hurt us, precious. Cruel little Hobbitses jumps on us like cats on poor mices. Gollum. We'll be nice to them if they'll be nice to us, won't we, precious?

SAM: Pity Mr Bilbo didn't kill the creature when he had the chance.

FRODO: I will not touch him. Now that I see him, I do pity him.

GOLLUM: Yes, Hobbits won't kill us, nice Hobbits, huh?

FRODO: No, we won't! But we won't let you go either! You will have to come with us and help us, if you can.

GOLLUM: Oooh yes, yes indeed. Nice Hobbits! And where are they going in these cold hard lands, we wonder?

FRODO: We are going to Mordor, Gollum. You know that!

casting. Once again, his principal intention was realism: 'I've treated it as a totally realistic film, all the characters are designed and drawn that way. The surroundings and some of the things that happen may be fantastic but I [want] the audience to relate strongly to the characters.' Casting the right voice was an essential part of getting the audience to empathize with the characters.

Voicing animation is one of the few acting jobs where the star system resolutely doesn't apply. As animation is such a stylized form, it's imperative that the voice blends in with the other elements in the film. No matter how big the name, if the voice doesn't fit, it doesn't go into the film. A bad performance, even if it's by the most famous star in the world, will strike a wrong note that can destabilize a film. If anything, casting an animated film is actually harder and more important than a live-action one. Voices are recorded sometimes years in advance of the film's completion so that artists can match drawings to lip movements, and a good performance will influence animators, who incorporate aspects of the performance into their drawings. (The best example of this in recent years is Robin Williams's performance as the Genie in *Aladdin*, where his improvising was carefully edited and worked into the film by animators who altered the character's performance according to his ad-libs.)

Bakshi claimed that he approached the cream of British acting talent to voice the major characters in the film, the three legendary theatrical knights – Olivier, Gielgud and Richardson. The eventual cast contained fewer distinguished names but was peopled by actors who, Bakshi felt, better embodied the characters. At the time, the cast was mostly unknown (although John Hurt was poised for stardom) and all were British, which was in keeping with the overall conception of the film but necessitated expensive trips to London to record the voices.

For Peter Beagle (and most of the contemporary critics), the casting is the most successful aspect of *The Lord of the Rings*: 'The best of Bakshi came out when he was dealing with the actors. From John Hurt to the Guard brothers, to Tony Daniels and Michael Graham Cox, they clearly respected him and responded well to his suggestions. I remember the recording sessions as the best part of the adventure.' Of the cast, Beagle singles out Peter Woodthorpe's slimy Gollum: 'We hit it off very well, and every time I caught him playing the police pathologist on *Inspector Morse*, I used to wave.'

The most controversial aspect of the production was Bakshi's decision to Rotoscope the entire film from live-action footage. Rotoscoping was a technique developed in the pioneering days of animation by the Fleischer brothers, Dave and Max, who were Walt Disney's principal rivals until he gained a stranglehold on the industry. It had traditionally been used by animators to beat their budgets down to a level acceptable to the financiers, and this was why Bakshi had been forced to use it initially.

But as Bakshi kept reminding interviewers, *The Lord of the Rings* wasn't affected by any of the budgetary constraints that had hampered his earlier films. For the first time in his entire career, he had a producer sympathetic and, more importantly, powerful enough to give him the freedom he had always wanted. (The film's final cost was $7.5 million.) And it was this freedom that allowed him the opportunity to finally consummate his obsession of merging the 'real' live-action image and the 'synthetic' animated one.

Although Bakshi had been developing the philosophy of integrating live action and animation throughout his films, the audacious decision to make *The Lord of the Rings* the first entirely Rotoscoped film came only after a lengthy period of experimentation, itself a luxury to the director: 'There are some things that are just impossible in pure animation, like having a lot of stuff going on at the same time. If an animator has to draw one character, it takes him so long; if he has to draw two, it will take him twice as long...if a guy has to draw 200 people in a scene, it will take him the rest of his life. So I started with the live action, just horses, and I shot that and it really worked, better than I thought it would. Then I decided to shoot the action of the main characters, running, jumping, falling, fighting. And I shot a couple of those and they were staggeringly good. Then the light bulb went off and I realized that the other big problem I was wrestling with was the structure. When an animation director starts to cut a film on storyboards, he instinctively eliminates what can't be done. You just write the shot out of the picture. I started to do that a *lot*. Directorially, it was like I was cheating every scene.

'Two years ago, the level of animation and the quality of realism I was after were not living up to the stuff I had shot. I'd have these great horses charging to a stop and these animated characters getting off and walking. One was beautiful and pure and realistic, and the other was *cartooning*. And then I went home at night worried, nervous, anxious…and then I realized, things in motion tend to keep in motion. Why don't I shoot the whole movie in live action?

'*Rings* is a tremendous walk away from what is traditional animation, a tremendous leap forward. On the other hand, so is Tolkien a tremendous leap forward. The approach in *Rings* was for pure realism, for believability of characters like Aragorn, for horses, that these things would not be caricatured.'

Bakshi's decision to Rotoscope the entire film meant that he had to provide material for his animators to trace over. This meant that he had to shoot the entire film as live-action first, before any actual drawing could be done. This required another 'casting' session, to find people to embody the action. Most importantly, he needed to find actors of a suitable size to play the film's Hobbits and so he turned to Billy Barty, with whom he had worked before. Barty was an actor, entertainer and founder of the Little People of America, an organization dedicated to representing the rights of midgets.

As well as being a great personality who left an indelible impression on people who worked with him, Barty was an impassioned campaigner for disabled rights and was fearsome in confronting the myths about little people, determined to present them as human beings and not exhibits at circus side-shows. He was always keen to get his organization involved in any project where little people could be presented as heroes. Bakshi remembers working with the Little People of America: 'They were all very excited. They'd read all the books and because Hobbits are small people and heroic, and the parts midgets play are usually unheroic, I couldn't get them off the set. They didn't want to quit because they were playing heroes. Not funny heroes, not goofy

THE RESURRECTION OF GANDALF

The old man approaches Gimli, Aragorn and Legolas, letting his hood fall and revealing his true form.

ARAGORN: Gandalf! Beyond all hope! Gandalf!

GANDALF: Yes... Yes, that was my name.

ARAGORN: But where have you... Gandalf! What happened?

GANDALF: Long time I fell. Long I fell and he fell with me. His fire was about me. I was burned. Ever he clutched me, and ever I hewed him, far under the living earth, until at last he fled up the secret ways of Moria. There we fought above the mists of the world and the mountain was wreathed with lightning. I threw down my enemy and his fall broke the mountainside. Then darkness took me and I wandered far on roads that I will not tell. Naked, I was sent back for a brief time until my task was done. And it is time I was about it! You must come with me to Edoras, my friends – to the city of the riders!

heroes, but heroes with capes on.' (Barty took the role of Bilbo; Frodo was played by Sharon Baird.)

The action was staged as plainly as possible, played against a bare white wall. This simplicity, required to make the Rotoscoping process as clear as possible, was hard on the actors, who had no points of reference. Bakshi himself found that shooting could sometimes be a chore: 'I'd do my storyboards in the morning, block out my scene so I knew where *I* was first. Then I put my simple props accordingly and kept referring back to my storyboards. It was difficult for the actors to get orientated.' Most of the film was 'shot' in America, but it was decided to shift 'production' to Spain for the complicated battle scenes, where the locations matched the images in Bakshi's head. This proved easier for the director to coordinate: 'I had points of reference – there was a castle to attack. I knew where to go and where to come from – [it was] much easier than shooting in a white room, where everything becomes infinite.'

But despite the effect that this technique gave the film, it also created difficulties that had not been foreseen in pre-production. Specifically, the problem was motion blurs. Sometimes movements are too quick for the camera to capture and consequently there is a loss of fine detail; the human eye doesn't notice this in live action but it suddenly becomes accentuated if that footage is Rotoscoped. 'When horses come charging by the camera and you look at the photographs and they blur, there's nothing there,' comments Bakshi. 'When masses of men are moving, your eye picks up the details but the camera does not; they kind of blend into an overall grey. Fast feet – feet moving very fast, too close to the camera, distort.'

Reshoots were impossible and so Bakshi had to 'reshoot' in the animation studio. This was partially achieved by throwing the blurred areas into heavy shadow and increasing the contrast. This is especially evident in the battle scenes. Bakshi and his editor also increased the speed of the cuts during the Battle of Helm's Deep to disguise it further. By accentuating shadow tone, the film was given two distinctive types of animation – one that looks like traditional cartooning and one that looks much more photorealistic. (The contrast of the foreground and background characters at the Prancing Pony inn shows the distinction most clearly.) Ultimately, the problem was effectively camouflaged and the action flows clearly and naturally.

As Bakshi hoped, the technique did indeed break new ground. Using live action allowed him to incorporate certain techniques into animation for the first time, like slow motion, playing with audience perceptions to better influence emotions. It also imbued the figures in *The Lord of the Rings* with a greater range of body language, as animators were able to capture the tiny twitches and gestures that rarely figure in conventional animation, creating a much greater sense of movement in the characters.

Having completed the major creative aspects of the project, Bakshi now needed to recruit a team of animators who would convert his footage into animation cels. For the first time, he was able to hire a decent number of staff and pay them a living wage. Rather than scout around for artists schooled in the traditional techniques he was kicking against, he placed an advertisement in *Variety* offering 'creative careers' to young artists. Some 25,000 replied to fill 600 places, according to Bakshi. Ever the meritocrat, he chose for ability rather than experience: 'I judge an individual on the basis of how well he draws. If the drawings are there, well, I set the standard of quality and they simply come up to it…I'm not sure you need to have great amounts of experience to animate successfully anyway, just talent. What makes animators go is a director or producer with a vision.'

To supervise these youngsters, senior animator Dale Baer was appointed to ensure consistency across the film. 'The most important thing is that a character does not change in a picture. I cast animators to play specific roles,' said Bakshi. Sometimes the old pros at his studio were resistant to his innovations, but the kids always played ball. The animation was completed in a little less than two years. The additional budget gave Bakshi another luxury he was unused to: the opportunity to have another pass if a shot failed to work. Previously his budgets had been so low that a failed shot had to be excised rather than redrawn.

The final addition to the film came from Leonard Rosenman,

hired by Bakshi and Zaentz to supply the rousing soundtrack. Rosenman had won an Oscar® for his work on Stanley Kubrick's *Barry Lyndon* and was a veteran of films like *East of Eden* and *Rebel Without a Cause*. For *The Lord of the Rings*, Rosenman supplied the strident Wagner-influenced score. After his experience in the record industry, Saul Zaentz took a special interest in recording the soundtrack, realizing that it was a marketable commodity in itself. Despite the plethora of songs in the book, only one finally made it through, an Elvish piece very different from Tolkien's conception of Elvish singing as 'like Gregorian chants'. With the completion of the score, production on Ralph Bakshi's biggest project was finished, ready for release.

THE RELEASE

Even after two and a half years and 250,000 individually painted images, Ralph Bakshi and Saul Zaentz had still not finished their work on *The Lord of the Rings*. They had to respond to suggestions as the picture was previewed, administer a marketing campaign and, if necessary, protect the film from any unwanted advances made by the studio distributing it.

The very first screening that United Artists arranged was, as Bakshi freely admits, disastrous: 'I was told that all the critics from Chicago to the West Coast were being invited to see this film. I hadn't had a sneak preview. So I went to the screening. And it didn't work. The people – the average age was about fifty-five or sixty, they were the right people for *Hollywood*. We went to a party after and there was this Frodo made out of chicken liver. It was like a bar mitzvah and people were dancing the foxtrot...Everyone smiling and telling me what a *wooonderful* film it was...I saw things in the film that I didn't like. And I started talking to myself about that. Some of the critics saw it, but they couldn't see past the non-reaction [of the audience]. [This] film was made for young people, Tolkien fans and my audience. The audience that saw *Fritz the Cat* is the same audience I made *Rings* for.'

The process was repeated on the East Coast for the New York critics, again with a similarly inappropriate audience, and Bakshi's doubts escalated. This wasn't the audience who could tell him if he'd made a good film or not. The increased budget and the prestige of the material had taken him away from his natural constituency. The audiences who were passing judgement now were a bad barometer for a Bakshi picture: 'They had never seen an animated feature and 99 per cent of them had never read Tolkien...There was no reaction again and everyone [at the studio]

In the cave Theoden is mounted on his steed, a king again.

ARAGORN: Theoden King.

THEODEN: I will not end here, taken like an old badger in a trap. When dawn comes, I will sound Helm's horn and I will ride forth. Will you ride with me then, son of Arathorn? At least we may make such an end as will be worth a song.

ARAGORN: I will ride with you.

was getting nervous...I said, "Wait a minute, Ralph, this is *real*.'"

Collaborators can attest to Bakshi's tenacity. Faced with the imminent scuppering of a film he'd poured heart and soul into, he rallied: 'After a long discussion with United Artists, they finally threw a paying sneak [preview] for me.' This film was one of the most eagerly awaited of the year. The book and the director had substantial cult followings and the film was being tracked by both groups, anxious to see a film that promised to be something very different. UA placed a single advertisement in the press and watched open-mouthed as the screening it promoted sold out. The 1,200 seats were snapped up and, Bakshi claims, the event was oversubscribed by 800. This was the audience he wanted. The lights dimmed and...

'The kids tore the house apart. They screamed, they yelled, they reacted, they jumped. Ninety-five per cent were Tolkien fans. I knew I was home when I entered the theater. The pinball machines were banging away like crazy and there was pot in the air and I knew at least I had the right audience...Now I'll finally get the right answer. Their reaction was more than I would ever dream for.' Bakshi and the executives who had accompanied him to the screening to gauge the reaction were all smiles: 'I felt I had reached the Tolkien fans, the people the picture was made for. I don't care about reviews. I find them interesting and I read them. I didn't get a bad review from someone who saw it with the right audience.'

The film was scheduled for a limited release in winter 1978, spreading wider early in 1979, and United Artists were optimistic about its chances of success. In between Bakshi gaining the rights and completing the film, a film called *Star Wars* had opened. Fantasy was now big business and not simply the preserve of a small minority. Despite the cross-over potential that UA now hoped for, they realized that they couldn't afford to neglect the film's core audience. Until *Star Wars*, the box-office pattern set by most fantasy films (sword and sorcery, science fiction) had been for a large opening before receipts declined sharply. It was therefore imperative to alert the fans of fantasy film early, to maximize profits in the first weeks of release, just in case the crossover miracle failed to occur.

Selling *The Lord of the Rings* had therefore begun before the film had even been completed. UA came up with a few morsels to tempt potential viewers: a slide show was coordinated, complete with a display of artwork from the film. This was taken around the science-fiction convention circuit, the natural habitat of the vanguard audience the studio was trying to woo. Predictably, this brief glimpse piqued the interest of convention-goers and left them hungry for more.

Despite the head start needed, marketing genre films is actually easier than marketing a film intended for broad mainstream consumption. The large, pre-existing audience was plugged into a vast network even before the days of the Internet. They attended sci-fi conventions, hotbeds of rumour that allowed easy dissemination of information, and there was a broad selection of extremely well-informed specialist magazines which carried frequent reports and updates about desirable films. UA had been tracking interest in *The Lord of the Rings* among this community for a while and knew that anticipation levels were high, but the reaction that they received when they began to promote the film seriously surprised even them.

One of the tried and tested methods of drumming up interest in a genre film was the give-away, whereby movie merchandising was given to fans, creating an interest. Usually a poster was chosen. Not only would it look 'cool' on the fan's wall, it was also good free advertising to anyone who saw it. The studio had done this sort of thing before. On the remake of *King Kong*, they invited fans to write in for a poster and were bombarded by 6,000 requests. For *The Lord of the Rings*, an ad was placed in newspapers in August in the cities where the picture would open in December. UA then crossed their fingers, hoping to do better than demand for *King Kong*...

Some 200,000 posters later, they realized they had something potentially very big on their hands. The poster give-away was the biggest promotional campaign ever seen in the film industry by three times. It had even eclipsed the early demand for *Star Wars* (although it should be noted that *Star Wars* wasn't based on a pre-existing franchise with an in-built fan base). The hype machine was warmed up and ready to go.

Trailers were produced and full-page colour advertisements were placed, going beyond the genre audience for the first time and targeting a mainstream crowd, readers of such magazines as *TV Guide*, *Time*, *Newsweek*, *Rolling Stone* and *The New Yorker*. Radio spots were booked in the cities where the picture would open and, to narrate them, UA hired Orson Welles, the prospective star of so many unmade versions. Saul Zaentz's showmanship also came into play. In the Macy's Thanksgiving Day parade, he booked a *Lord of the Rings* float, three storeys high, belching fire and accompanied by riders on horseback. National TV covered the event and pictures of the float appeared in newspapers, costing the producer a fraction of the price of a TV commercial and commanding considerably more exposure.

With the film almost in cinemas, the merchandising began to hit the shelves. After the runaway success of *Star Wars* tie-ins, companies had realized what a cash cow movies could be and Saul Zaentz was happy to help them milk it. His purchase of the merchandising rights two years earlier now looked extremely astute. First in line to seek licences were the makers of such regular movie tie-ins as greetings cards, storybooks and games of the film. But licences were granted for the manufacture of towels and bedlinen branded with the film's logo as well. Zaentz also managed to arrange some more exclusive contracts, such as a Kingmaker chess set based on characters from the film and Royal Doulton china figurines.

His background in the music industry led him to be especially proactive with the soundtrack. Its release was the first and best indication of the film's success before the film actually opened. Leonard Rosenman's music went on sale in early November, a month before the film premiered, and sold well enough to enter all three national charts. By the time the film was released, the record had gone gold and, as the film spread, it went platinum.

Interest was at fever pitch among fans, but before they could see it the film would be screened again for the critics and their verdicts published. Good notices were important if the film was to reach beyond the core audience who had ordered the poster, were listening to the LP and resting their heads on a *Lord of the Rings* pillowcase. The film's luck continued as it received the best notices of any Bakshi film, with critics praising his 'imagination' and the 'fine' cast. Even though he professed not to worry about them, Bakshi was relieved the worst the critics could accuse him of was overlooking those who had not read the books.

Surveying an illustrious career in 1998, a career that had earned him Oscars and a personal fortune, Saul Zaentz was asked what his biggest professional disappointment was. He replied that it was *The Lord of the Rings*: 'We didn't make as good a picture as we could have made, not nearly as good as we could have made. It made money and everything, but it wasn't the right picture. You try and find out what went wrong, but often these things are intangible so you never know.'

Zaentz obviously doesn't exclude himself from what he sees as the 'failure' of *The Lord of the Rings*. He was, after all, intimately involved with the development of the film and participated in many key creative decisions, such as how to structure the project. Perhaps his recollection of the film has been coloured by the successes he was involved with in the 1980s and 1990s. Certainly he was considerably more positive about the film at the time. In an interview given two weeks after the film was released, the producer was positively purring.

The opening weekend had proved even more successful than United Artists had dared hope. Despite playing on only thirty-two screens in twenty-two cities, it had already earned well over $3 million. 'That's an amazing average of around $30,000 per theater,' glowed the satisfied Zaentz. He continued, 'United Artists is now projecting a minimum of $50 million [domestic gross]. They put out a story that it is the biggest opening in the history of UA, which includes some pretty big films.' Asked about his production partner on *One Flew Over the Cuckoo's Nest*, actor Michael Douglas, Zaentz replied with a grin, 'We saw him Friday night and he wanted to know if he could buy a piece of it now.'

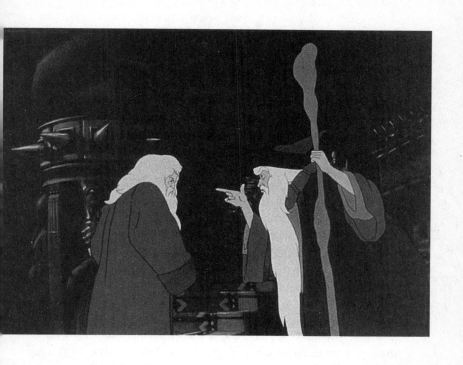

In the first month, *everyone* wanted to buy a piece of *The Lord of the Rings*. One of the most persistent myths about the film is that it flopped. In fact, it was a considerable success, but it failed to overwhelm audiences in the way that UA had hoped, making their box-office predictions look dramatically over-optimistic. In fact, despite the early prognostications, the film repeated the pattern familiar to genre films. It gained a strong core audience who gave it a huge opening but it didn't cross over to the mainstream crowd that was needed for it to make serious money.

A post-mortem on the film would show its potential was hobbled by the runaway success of Warner Brothers' *Superman*. The super-hero epic was the season's box-office locomotive and had picked up an unstoppable momentum that drew audiences away from all other films, including *The Lord of the Rings*. United Artists' advertising campaign should share some of the blame, as it failed to mention that the film was only 'Part One'. Audiences were shocked when the film they had been enjoying ended so abruptly, with no apparent warning. Bakshi had never hidden the fact he was working on two films, but the marketing suits feared the commitment that meant would deter audiences and declined to publicize the fact. As it was, their chicanery led to a certain amount of negative word of mouth from cinema-goers angry at the deception.

By its final appearance in the *Variety* box-office chart in 1979, eighteen weeks after it opened, the film had earned $6,774,884 in rentals (i.e. money back to the distributor as opposed to gross profit) and was still playing on sixty-two screens. Although not in the chart, it continued to play and eventually cleared $10 million (a more than respectable figure at 1979 ticket prices). A similar pattern was repeated across the world as the picture was rolled out. Although never the runaway success that the early figures indicated, it did solid business everywhere it played.

The supposed box-office failure of the first part of *The Lord of the Rings* is the reason most often given for the non-appearance of Part Two. In fact, the film had done well enough to justify producing a sequel. Although the box office wasn't as large as was hoped, Bakshi could demonstrate that a follow-up would have a built-in audience. Having used the first film as an opportunity to experiment and innovate, a second film using proven techniques and staff members familiar with them would be a cheaper investment. The reasons why Bakshi never completed the second part of *The Lord of the Rings* are more complicated.

As the film was released, Bakshi had already begun work on his next project, another semi-autobiographical film, *American Pop*. This was a move away from the fantasy of his most recent films (*Wizards* and *The Lord of the Rings*) and a return to the street style that he was best known for. There was also talk of him directing a live-action film (entitled *If I Catch Her, I'll Kill Her*), which would add to the delay. Although Bakshi was still keen to finish *The Lord of the Rings*, it wasn't his priority. Without encouragement, there was a danger it might slip off the agenda altogether.

Meanwhile, United Artists were having troubles of their own. The top-level executives, widely regarded as some of the best in the business, had quarrelled with the board and had subsequently left the company to establish their own mini-studio, Orion Pictures. To fill the vacuum left by their departure, less experienced executives were promoted to positions they were unprepared for. This new guard bankrolled a series of films that performed disastrously at the box office. Most notably, the team gave the green light to *Heaven's Gate*. Regardless of the film's artistic success, it earned a reputation as the all-time box-office dud and became infamous as the film that sank a studio. UA had poured almost all their available resources into *Heaven's Gate* and when it flopped, the studio was forced into a merger with MGM.

Caught between a director busy with a raft of other projects (although *If I Catch Her, I'll Kill Her* failed to appear, other projects suggested themselves to fill Bakshi's time) and a studio only interested in sure-fire blockbusters (such as its James Bond movies and the sequels to *Rocky*), the second part of *The Lord of the Rings* never happened. There was no one to lobby for it and so ultimately it was never made. The fans waited patiently but eventually it became apparent that the wait was futile and rumours began circulating to explain why.

A sequel of sorts was produced by the team at Rankin/Bass, using the TV rights they had clung on to despite pressure from the studio. Their version of *The Return of the King* was a spoiler operation, rushed into production to capitalize on Bakshi's film and shown on TV in 1980. It used the same cast (including John Huston as Gandalf) and the same chocolate-box animation style as their earlier cartoon version of *The Hobbit*. It has acquired a respectability among certain Tolkien fans that it demonstrably does not deserve.

The legal and financial troubles created by the collapse of United Artists restricted the availability of Ralph Bakshi's film for many years. Sporadic television showings and limited availability on home video have created a thriving black market in badly duplicated cassettes sold at conventions and through the small ads. The rise of the Internet expanded this marketplace world-wide (and created a dramatic hike in prices). Copies of the legitimate video release sold for hundreds of pounds in the early days of eBay, although they have fallen in price since then.

Happily, with the film back in circulation cultists can finally purchase their own good-quality copies. Unlike with many cult films, fans of *The Lord of the Rings* remain unobtrusive, but there are more of them than even they may think. Bakshi's film has routinely been dismissed but it holds up well as a deeply personal and uncompromising interpretation of one of the most subjective books ever written. Moreover, as the fan base testifies, there are a lot of people who think his vision works brilliantly. Outside the circle of Tolkien fans, the inventive animation has many admirers. Remember, this is Bakshi unshackled by budgetary constraints and many animation fans watch it to see him at the height of his imagination.

The Lord of the Rings is not a film that will ever be universally popular but it is one that deserves more than the grudging praise it is awarded at present. A bold reading of a difficult book, Bakshi's film is evidence of the effort he poured into the project. No matter how many subsequent film versions are made, his will always have the distinction of being the first and, for many fans, the best.

NARRATOR: The forces of darkness were driven for ever from the face of Middle Earth by the valiant friends of Frodo. As their gallant battle ended, so too ends the first great tale of The Lord of the Rings.

Closing narration to The Lord of the Rings

CAST LIST AND CREDITS

Directed by Ralph Bakshi
Produced by Saul Zaentz
Screenplay by Chris Conkling and Peter S. Beagle
(Based on the novels by J. R. R. Tolkien)
Director of Photography Timothy Galfas
Music Composed and Conducted by Leonard Rosenman
Edited by Donald W. Ernst, ACE
Assistant Director John Sparey
Studio Production Supervisor Jacqueline Roettcher
Animation Production Supervisor Daniel Pia
Assistants to the Director Lynne Betner, Leah Bernstein
Assistant to the Producer Nancy Eichler
Layout Dale Baer, Louise Zingarelli, Mentor Huebner, David
Jonas, Mike Ploog, Kevin Hanna
Landscapes Painted by Barry Jackson, Johnnie Vita, Marcia
Adams, Edwin B. Hirth III, Carol Kieffer
Background Assistants Lou Police, J. Michael Spooner, Ira Turk
Key Animators Craig Armstrong, Dale Baer, Brenda Banks, Carl
Bell, Jesus Cortes, Lillian Evans, Frank Gonzales, Steven Gordon,
Sean Joyce, Lenord Robinson, Chrystal Russell, Paul Smith, Irven
Spence, Hank Tucker, Edward Wexler, Bruce Woodside, James
A. Davis
Animators Sam Jaimes, Manny Perez, Joe Roman, Phil Roman,
Martin Tara
Assistant Animators Retta Davidson, Charlotte Huffine, Rob La
Doca, Terrence Lennon, Edward Newman, Barry Temple
Colour Model Janet Cummings
Animation Effects Stan Green, Nino Carbe, Christopher
Andrews

Ink and Special Effects Mary Jane Cole, Ann Hamilton, Linda Pearce, Emaline Seutter, Karin Stover

Ink and Paint Supervisors Janet Cummings, Vince Gutierrez, Lee Guttman, Lisa Kshatriya, Sally Redmond, Nelda Ridley, Ruth Tompson, Micki Zurcher

Animation Checker Dotti Foell

Cel Reproductions Edgar Gutierrez

Production Staff Mark Bakshi, Martin Cohen, Christine L. Danzo, Jacquelyn Herst, Cathy Rose, Michael Takamato

Still Photographer Phil Bray

Animation Camera Nick Vasu Inc., R&B EFX & Animation, Hogan-Lee Images

Negative Cutters Jack Hooper, Tom Hooper

Sound Effects Sam Shaw Enterprises

Assistant Sound Editors Daniel Sharp, Cari Lewis

Special Kaleidoscopic Effect by Symmetricon

Music Editor Jim Henrikson

Editor Peter Kirby

Re-recording Bill Varney, Bob Minkler, Bill Mumford

Dolby Consultant Stephen Katz

Optical Effects by The Optical House, LA

Title Design Wayne Fitzgerald

Special Costumes Designed and Constructed by William Barbe and Lynn Betner

Orchestration by Ralph Ferraro

Song 'MITHRANDIR' Music by Leonard Rosenman and words by Mark Fleischer

CAST

With the Voices of

FRODO Christopher Guard
GANDALF William Squire
SAM Michael Scholes
ARAGORN John Hurt
MERRY Simon Chandler
PIPPIN Dominic Guard
BILBO Norman Bird
BOROMIR Michael Graham-
  Cox
LEGOLAS Anthony Daniels
GIMLI David Buck
GOLLUM Peter Woodthorpe
(S)ARUMAN Fraser Kerr
THEODEN Philip Stone
WORMTONGUE Michael
  Deacon
ELROND Andre Morell
INNKEEPER Alan Tilvern
GALADRIEL Annette Crosbie
TREEBEARD John Westbrook

Character Actors
Sharon Baird
Paul Gale
Billy Barty
Trey Wilson
Patty Maloney
Felix Silla
Larry Larsen
David Dotson
and
Aesop Aquarian
Stan Barrett
Herb Braha
Patrick Sullivan Burke

Hank Calia
Albert Cirimele
Mike Clifford
Frank Delfino
Russ Earnest
Louis Elias
Carmen Filipi
Ruth Gay
Lenny Gear
Harriett Gibson
Michael Lee Gogin
Bob Haney
Chuck Hayward
Art Hern
Eddie Hice
Loren Janes
Gary Jensen
Santy Josol
John L.
Sam Laws
Terry Leonard
Peter Looney
Dennis Madalone
Tommy Madden
Buck Maffei
Jerry Maren
Harry Monty
Frank Morson
John A. Neris
Jeri Lea Ray
Walt Robles
Mic Rodgers
Angelo Rossitto
Pete Risch
Jack Verbois
Gregg Walker
Donn Whyte

Other important *ScreenPress* titles to accompany *Warner Bros.* films:

A CLOCKWORK ORANGE
A unique illustrated screenplay containing over 800 still images from *Stanley Kubrick's A Clockwork Orange*, selected by Kubrick when the film was first released in 1971. A fascinating and unmatched book – a must for all interested in this most uncompromising of British films.
ISBN 1 901680 47 9
Soft-bound, 340 pages, illustrated throughout
£14.99

GET CARTER
This brilliant writing and directing debut from Mike Hodges is perhaps the greatest British gangster film ever made, truly a cult classic, unprecedented in terms of style and visual inventiveness. Despite containing some of the most quoted dialogue ever spoken on film, this screenplay has never previously been available in print.
ISBN 1 901680 32 0
Soft-bound, 128 pages, illustrated throughout
£7.99

THE EXORCIST
If There Were Demons Then Perhaps There Were Angels is William Peter Blatty's own story of *The Exorcist*. Unavailable for over twenty years, this is the fully authorized account of how Blatty came to write both the novel and the screenplay of one of the most unsettling films ever made.
ISBN 1 901680 34 7
Soft-bound, 64 pages, illustrated with original line drawings
£4.99

ALL BOOKS ARE AVAILABLE ONLINE AT WWW.SCREENPRESS.CO.UK